D1088381

6199

CÉLINE DION

A Real-Life Reader Biography

Melanie Cole

Mitchell Lane Publishers, Inc.
P.O. Box 200 • Childs, Maryland 21916

Second Printing
Real-Life Reader Biographies

Selena	Robert Rodriguez	Mariah Carey	Rafael Palmeiro
Tommy Nuñez	Trent Dimas	Cristina Saralegui	Andres Galarraga
Oscar De La Hoya	Gloria Estefan	Jimmy Smits	Mary Joe Fernandez
Cesar Chavez	Chuck Norris	Sinbad	Paula Abdul
Vanessa Williams	**Celine Dion**	Mia Hamm	Shania Twain
Sammy Sosa	Brandy	Garth Brooks	Jeff Gordon

Library of Congress Cataloging-in-Publication Data
Cole, Melanie, 1957–
    Céline Dion / Melanie Cole.
      p. cm. (A real-life reader biography)
    Includes index.
    Summary: A biography of the French Canadian girl, youngest of fourteen siblings, who has become an international singing sensation.
    ISBN 1-883845-76-9
    1. Dion, Céline—Juvenile literature. 2. Singers—Canada—Biography—Juvenile literature. [1. Dion, Céline. 2. Singers. 3. Women—Biography.] I. Title. II. Series.
ML3930.D47C65 1998
782.42164'092—dc21
[B]   98-30686
                                                                                      CIP
                                                                                   AC MN

ABOUT THE AUTHOR: Melanie Cole has been a writer and editor for eighteen years. She was previously an associate editor of *Texas Monthly* and then an editor of *Hispanic* magazine. She has published numerous poems, articles, and reviews. She is a contributing writer to the Mitchell Lane series **Famous People of Hispanic Heritage** and has authored several books for children, including **Mary Joe Fernandez** (Mitchell Lane) and **Jimmy Smits** (Mitchell Lane). Originally from Kansas, Ms. Cole now resides in Austin, Texas.
PHOTO CREDITS: cover: Steve Finn/Globe Photos, taken at the 1996 World Music Awards; p. 4 courtesy Sony Music; p. 8 courtesy Céline Dion; p. 17 Mark Allan/Globe Photos; p. 21 Ron Davis/Shooting Star; p. 26 AP Photos; p. 29 Ron Davis/Shooting Star
ACKNOWLEDGMENTS: The following story has been thoroughly researched, and to the best of our knowledge, represents a true story. Though we try to authorize every biography that we publish, for various reasons, this is not always possible.

Table of Contents

Chapter 1
Tiny Singer, Big Voice

From the time she was a young girl, Céline Dion's single focus in life has been music. The only thing she ever wanted to do was to be a singer. Céline comes from a large, musical family. As a young girl, she sang for and entertained her brothers, sisters, *maman,* and *papa* in the little town in Quebec, Canada, where she grew up. Quebec is a province of Canada whose official language is French. Céline was named after a song—a Quebec hit

Céline Dion comes from a large, musical family.

called "Dis-Moi Céline" ("Call Me Céline").

Céline was born on March 30, 1968, in Charlemagne, a town of 6,000 people 30 miles east of Montreal. She was the 14th child of Thérèse (Tanguay) and Adhémar Dion. Her large family was like many Catholic, French-speaking families in Quebec. Céline grew up singing and speaking French. Almost everyone in Charlemagne— 98 percent of the people—still speaks only French.

When Céline was little, she was always singing. She had plenty of role models, since all the Dion children and both parents were musically gifted. The family often performed folk songs together as a group. Céline remembered these musical roots and her drive to be a singer on the VH-1 show, *Céline*:

> **When Céline was little, she was always singing.**

"When I was five years old and I was singing on the kitchen table for my brothers and sisters, I was having the best time! Today, I'm still having the best time. Every single moment, I went for it one hundred percent."

Although Céline's parents were extremely poor, they were dedicated to their family. To save up to build their own house in Charlemagne, Thérèse and Adhémar pinched every penny. To save 40 cents a day, Adhémar walked instead of taking the bus to work. Not able to afford a carpenter, the couple decided to build their house with their own hands. Neighbors still remember how Thérèse Dion, pregnant with her seventh baby, would climb a ladder to help nail boards on the roof of the house.

"When I was five years old and I was singing on the kitchen table for my brothers and sisters, I was having the best time!"

Because music was always part of the family, Adhémar and Thérèse decided to try to make a living from music. With so many children to tend to, Céline's mother had her hands full, but she always seemed able to do more. To support the family, Adhémar had worked as a butcher, a prison guard, and a factory worker. The family had gone on the road as a singing group, calling themselves the Dion Family. But soon after Céline was born,

Céline began her singing career at an early age. She was already an accomplished singer by age 12.

they got the idea of starting a family restaurant and piano bar. That way they could share their love of music with the community while making a living at the same time. Adhémar played the accordion, Thérèse the violin, and various brothers and sisters played guitar, bass, and drums and sang. They called the piano bar Le Vieux Baril (The Old Barrel).

Céline's first performance in public was at her brother Michel's wedding. Céline's sister Claudette said about her performance, "We were in awe about how amazing she was. It was at that point that we all knew she could become a famous singer."

Said Céline: "I never had the exact picture in my mind of how it was going to be, but I always knew I wanted to be a singer. I hope to sing for the rest of my life, because I really am sincerely happy to be able to do it."

Céline's first public per— formance was at her brother Michel's wedding.

Chapter 2
Canadian Sensation

When Céline was 12, her brother sent a demo tape she had made to a well-known Montreal-based agent named Rene Angélil. Angélil had been popular in the 1960s and '70s in Canada as the lead singer of a group called Les Baronets, a Quebec version of the Beatles. He represented other successful Quebec singers, including Ginette Reno and René Simard.

It took a long time for the musician-turned-agent to get to

Céline's tape because lots of young people were sending him demos, trying to be the next big star. After he heard Céline's song "It Was Only a Dream," he called her in for a visit. The song was an original; the words were written by her mother; the music was written by her brother Jacques. Jacques now has a musical career of his own under the name Jacques St. Clair.

On the day of their visit, Thérèse dressed Céline up in her nicest dress. She told her not to be nervous, to just be herself. At the agent's office, Céline pretended she was singing to an audience of friendly people. She held a pen to her mouth and pretended it was a microphone. "While I was singing, he started to cry," said Céline. "I knew then that I had done a good job."

Céline held a pen to her mouth and pretended she was singing into a micro—phone.

Beginning her profes— sional career at age 13, Céline was caught up in the world of music.

Rene thought she was so good that he decided to handle her career exclusively. Although he was having a hard time financially, he bet everything he had on the child singer. He mortgaged his house so that he could have enough money to finance Céline's first album. He told the girl and her mother, "Trust in me, and I'll make her a giant star within five years."

Beginning her professional career at age 13, Céline was caught up in the world of music. She kept singing her Quebec folk songs, taking them on the road with Rene and her mother. They toured Canada, Japan, and Europe. Because of the intense schedule, Céline dropped out of school at age 14. Her whole life was focused on singing and she didn't have time for anything else. "I had one dream: I wanted to be a singer," she said.

Under Angélil's guidance, Céline released her first French-language album, *La Vois du Bon Dieu*, and was well on the way to becoming a star in Canada. Since that time she has been affectionately called *la petite Québécoise* (the little Quebecker), the darling of the province of Quebec.

Because Céline was the youngest Dion child, her *maman* was able to travel with her and be her guide and chaperone until she turned 18. Céline's mother guided her through these first years as a young professional singer. Céline says she owes much of her success to the support of her mother.

"I had one dream," she said. "I wanted to be a singer."

Chapter 3
Chart Topper

Céline began to be noticed inter— nationally for her incredible voice in 1982.

From 1982 through 1985, with her vocal gifts and his experience in the music business, Céline and her manager Rene churned out nine albums in French. Seven were released in Quebec and two were released in France. She began to be noticed internationally for her incredible voice in 1982, when she won the gold medal at the Yamaha World Song Festival in Tokyo, Japan. That same year she also won a Musician's Award for top performer. In 1983, she became the first Canadian ever to receive a gold record in France.

Rene decided that since she had conquered Quebec, it was time to conquer the United States. To do that, Céline would have to move away from her girlish look and learn English. At the age of 18, she took a crash Berlitz course in English and released her first album in English. Like anyone who learns a new language, Céline was at first very nervous. As her English improved, her delivery of songs became stronger.

In 1989, Céline signed a deal with Epic Records, which would later spin off to become 550/Sony. Her first deal with the U.S. company resulted in the album *Unison*. Released in 1990, the album contained her first big U.S. hit, "Where Does My Heart Beat Now."

In 1989, Céline signed a deal with Epic Records to record an album for the U.S.

Céline's big break-through came in 1992 when she sang the theme from *Beauty and the Beast* with Peabo Bryson.

Céline's biggest breakthrough came in 1992. That year she sang the song that made her a U.S. star: the theme from *Beauty and the Beast,* with Peabo Bryson. It went to number one and won a Grammy Award (the U.S. music industry's highest prize) and an Academy Award (the U.S. movie industry's highest prize). The song was also included on Céline's second English album, called *Céline Dion.* Other hits on that album were "Love Can Move Mountains," "If You Asked Me To," and "Water from the Moon."

With the 1993 release of *The Colour of My Love,* Céline established herself as a major recording artist. This album included the hit song from the movie *Sleepless in Seattle,* a duet she sang with British vocalist Clive

Griffin, called "When I Fall in Love."

One of the things that makes Céline a strong performer is that she adapts her great singing ability to the studio, live performances, and videos. But it wasn't always smooth

Céline is a strong performer who can entertain almost any audience.

sailing. One night in 1990, she was getting ready to sing at an important concert, and when she opened her mouth, nothing came

> **"When I lost my voice, it was like losing my life."**

out. Céline rushed to a Montreal doctor, who prescribed surgery. But surgery was known to be a risky procedure. Sometimes the vocal cords don't bounce back. Both Céline and Rene were worried that her career could be over. They sought a second opinion from a New York throat specialist, Dr. Gwen Korovin. She prescribed three weeks of rest and silence.

"Thank God it worked," Céline told *McCall's* magazine. "When I lost my voice, it was like losing my life. . . . It was a wake-up call to take better care of myself."

Chapter 4
International Diva

The word *diva* comes from the world of opera. It means the female lead singer, the prima donna, the star of the show. Much has been written about Céline's status among the other pop music divas of our time—Aretha Franklin, Whitney Houston, Mariah Carey, Gloria Estefan, and fellow Canadian Shania Twain. *Time* magazine featured Céline on their August 12, 1996, cover and in the story "Viva the Divas." *Time* writer Charles Alexander noted that modern-day

Céline has earned her right as an inter—national diva.

divas generally sing lush ballads and have amazing vocal gifts. He described Céline as the epitome of this type of female singer: "Dion is the very model of a modern global diva—and a record company's dream girl (Sony Music's dream girl, to be specific). In an era in which rock stars are increasingly irritable about interviews and tours, Dion will crisscross continents, perform every night, answer stupid questions, cut ribbons, or do whatever else it takes to get songs up the charts."

Céline emphasizes that all the touring and recording is what she lives for. "I don't wake up in the morning thinking, 'How many records have I sold today?' . . . I know that all these things are important, because it proves that it's all working. But I'm not a number. Deep in my heart, I didn't want a hit, I [wanted] a career," she told VH-1.

Céline gives of herself in other ways, besides her music, too. In 1993 she became a celebrity spokesperson for the Canadian Cystic Fibrosis Foundation. Cystic fibrosis is a disease that affects the lungs and digestive system. Céline's niece Karine Menard, the daughter of her sister Liette, was born with cystic fibrosis. When Karine was 16, she died from the disease. Céline is also involved with other charities, including the T.J. Martell Foundation and the Diana, Princess of Wales Memorial Fund.

Céline spread some rather surprising news in late 1993. She was going to marry her manager, Rene. At the time she announced their engagement—on the liner

In 1993, Céline married her manager, Rene Angélil.

notes to her album *The Colour of My Love*—she was 25 and he was 52. The two were married in a fairy-tale ceremony at Notre Dame Basilica in Montreal on December 17, 1994. It

was a traditional Catholic ceremony. Some of Céline's fans have worried about the difference in Céline's and Rene's ages. Céline has had only one other boyfriend in her life, for two weeks when she was a teenager. Rene was her mentor and manager, and now he was her husband.

Céline with husband-manager, Rene Angélil

Chapter 5
Competing
With Herself

Millions of television viewers watched the opening ceremonies of the 1996 Olympics in Atlanta. There, dressed in white and backed by a 300-member gospel choir, was Céline. She belted out a song that celebrated the Olympic spirit: "The Power of the Dream." The song was a triumphant moment for Céline. The words applied not only to the athletes in competition but also to Céline's drive to make it to the top.

Indeed, Céline's music is loved by people of all nations.

Céline sang for millions of viewers at the opening ceremonies of the 1996 Olympics.

"Connecting with my audience is as important as breathing," says Céline.

"Connecting with my audience is as important as breathing," Céline has said over and over again.

At the 1996 Academy Awards, Céline sang her Oscar-nominated song from *Up Close and Personal,* "Because You Loved Me." She also got the opportunity to sing a Barbra Streisand number. When she went onstage, she noticed Streisand in the audience. It was a chance to perform before one of her biggest idols. To Céline's horror, Streisand walked out during her performance. Streisand was angry at the Academy for having snubbed her by asking someone else to sing her song. Later, Streisand sent Céline an apology, saying she hadn't meant to be rude to her personally. After that, the two divas became good friends, recording the song "Tell Him" on Céline's *Let's*

Talk About Love album. "Tell Him" became a smash hit in 1998.

Céline loved working with Streisand. She told VH-1, "I can say to you that the person that I look up to the most in my life is my mother. But the person I look up to the most in show business—as an actress, as a singer definitely, as a woman—is Barbra Streisand."

After selling 8 million copies of *Falling Into You*, Céline was nominated for four Grammy Awards. Overall, by 1997 she had won three Grammys—best pop vocal by a duo or group in 1993 for "Beauty and the Beast," and both album of the year and pop album of the year in 1997 for *Falling Into You*. Besides winning the Grammys in the United States, she has won numerous Juno and Felix awards in

Falling Into You won a Grammy in 1997.

Céline Dion holds up her award after winning the Best Pop Album at the 39th Annual Grammy Awards in New York on February 26, 1997. She won for her album Falling Into You.

Canada and World Music Awards in Europe.

In 1998 Céline received two special honors from her country. The Canadian government awarded her the honorary title of Officer of the Order of Canada, which is bestowed upon prestigious Canadians. The governor general of Canada declared: "Through her recordings and accomplished performances, she consistently demonstrates the high regard she has for her audiences. This great artist is an example of drive and determination for all Canadians." That same month Céline received the Order of Quebec from her French-speaking homeland. Quebec's premier said as he pinned on the medal, "Here and around the world, you are the best-known and most admired Quebecker."

Céline says she owes her slim figure to an overactive metabolism. Though some have accused her of being anorexic, Céline says nothing can be farther from the truth. "I don't want people to hate me," she says, "but I can eat anything I want. I don't exercise, and every night in bed, I eat a big bag of chips."

She and Rene have tried to take time off from their extremely busy life to start a family. But it hasn't happened yet. Coming from such a large family, Céline longs to be a mother herself. She and Rene have

Céline says her slim figure comes from an overactive metabolism. She can eat anything she wants.

told the press publicly for the past three years that they are trying. When it happens, her *maman* will be the first to know—Céline calls her mother every day, no matter where in the world she might be. "My family is my foundation," Céline said. "We never had a lot of money, but we had a wealth of love, joy, and affection."

The family stays close in other ways. Her brother Michel and sisters Manon and Pauline both work with her. Michel is her assistant tour director, Manon is a wardrobe assistant, and Pauline is president of her fan club.

Céline's latest passion is golf. "It sounds kind of bizarre," she said to *USA Today.* "You hit a ball, you run after it, you hit it again, you run after it again. But to me, it's like show business. It's like focusing, and you are not in competition with the world, you are in competition with you! You want to beat your last performance, your last record." In a similar vein, she said on the VH-1 television special *Céline*, which showed highlights of her life and career, "I'm not in competition with anyone but myself. I want each album to be better than the last one."

On the professional front, she's at the top. She's done about everything a singer can do—released hit after hit, toured the world, sang at major venues like the Olympics, and shared the stage with veterans of the

Céline with fellow Canadian singer Shania Twain

> **"I have accomplished a lot and I don't want people to get tired of me," says Céline.**

entertainment industry. She has worked with singers she always admired, including Barbra Streisand, Frank Sinatra, and Shania Twain. Céline Dion is in their company as a full-fledged superstar.

What does Céline say about her future? "I have accomplished a lot and I don't want people to get tired of me. I don't want to stop my career completely. I'd love to do some acting, a concert once in awhile and maybe a TV special. But I also want to retire. I can't wait to go grocery shopping and drive my car."

Official Web site: www.Célineonline.com

Discography

Selected Top Singles

"Where Does My Heart Beat Now" (1990)

"Love Can Move Mountains" (1992)

"If You Asked Me To" (1992)

"Water From the Moon" (1992)

"Beauty and the Beast" from *Beauty and the Beast* (1993)

"When I Fall in Love," from *Sleepless in Seattle* (1994)

"Because You Loved Me" (1996)

"It's All Coming Back to Me Now" (1996)

"All By Myself" (1996)

"The Power of the Dream" Olympics theme song (1996)

"Tell Him" with Barbra Streisand (1997)

"My Heart Will Go On" from *Titanic* (1997)

Albums

In French

Melanie (1984)

C'est Pour Toi (1985)

Incognito (1987)

Les Premieres Années (1993)

D'eux (1995)

S'il Suffisait D'aimer (1998)

In English

Unison (1990)

Céline Dion (1992)

The Colour of My Love (1993)

Falling Into You (1996)

Gold, Volumes 1 & 2 (1996)

Let's Talk About Love (1997)

These Are Special Times (1998)

Chronology

- Born March 30, 1968, in Charlemagne, Quebec; mother Thérèse Tanguay Dion (b. 1927); father: Adhémar Dion (b. 1923)·
- Began singing professionally at age 13; released her first French-language album, *La Vois du Bon Dieu,* and became a star in Canada
- 1982–1985, churned out nine albums in French, seven in Quebec and two in France
- 1989, learned English and released her first album in English; signed a deal with Epic Records in 1989
- 1993, sang the song that made her a U.S. star: the theme from *Beauty and the Beast,* with Peabo Bryson; released the album *The Colour of My Love*
- 1994, married her manager, Rene Angélil
- Sang at the 1996 Olympic Games in Atlanta
- 1997, appeared at the Academy Awards, where she met her idol, Barbra Streisand
- 1998, became an Officer of the Order of Canada and of the Order of Quebec; released album, *These Are Special Times*, began world tour

Index